# Waste
# and Recycling

## Jen Green

Chrysalis Children's Books

First published in the UK in 2004 by
Chrysalis Children's Books
An imprint of Chrysalis Books Group plc
The Chrysalis Building, Bramley Road,
London W10 6SP

ISBN 1 84458 064 4

British Library Cataloguing in Publication Data for this
book is available from the British Library.

Editorial Manager: Joyce Bentley

Produced by Tall Tree Ltd
Designer: Ed Simkins
Editor: Kate Simkins
Consultant: Michael Rand
Picture Researcher: Lorna Ainger
Artwork: Hardlines Ltd
Printed in China

Some of the more unfamiliar words used in this book
are explained in the glossary on page 31.

Photo Credits:
Alamy/Lonnie Duka: front cover br, 27t, Ken Hawkins:
front cover c, 10, 30, David Hoffman: front cover c,
back cover, 6, Steve Skjold 5t,
Robert Battersby/Tografox 8, 9, 17b, 23t, 27b
Corbis/Jeff Albertson 20, James L. Amos 1, 22, Yann
Arthus-Bertrand 16, Tom Stewart 26, Natalie Fobes
23b, Gehl Company 14, Nick Hawkes/Ecoscene 15b,
Ed Kashi 13t, Rob Lewine 7b, Richard Hamilton Smith
11t, Getty Images/Hugh Burden 18
Ed Simkins 28t, Still Pictures/Mark Edwards: front cover
tr, 2, 11b, 17t, 21t, 31, Julio Etchart: front cover tl, 5b,
Peter Frischmuth 24, Gayo 15t, Philippe Hays 13b,
19b, Robert J. Ross 25t, Kevin Schafer 19t, Hartmut
Schwarzbach 4.

# Contents

# What a waste!

**E**very hour of every day, we produce waste as we eat, drink and go about our lives. The waste produced by everyone adds up to a huge amount. We have to get rid of this waste through a process called waste disposal.

Houses, schools, shops and offices all make waste. So do farms and factories. If waste is not disposed of safely, it can pollute nature and harm people and wildlife. As the number of people in the world increases, so the problem of waste disposal is growing, too. Waste can be in a solid form, such as rubbish, a liquid, such as dirty water, or a gas, such as carbon dioxide.

▼ As vehicles burn fuel, such as petrol, they also produce waste gases that pollute the air.

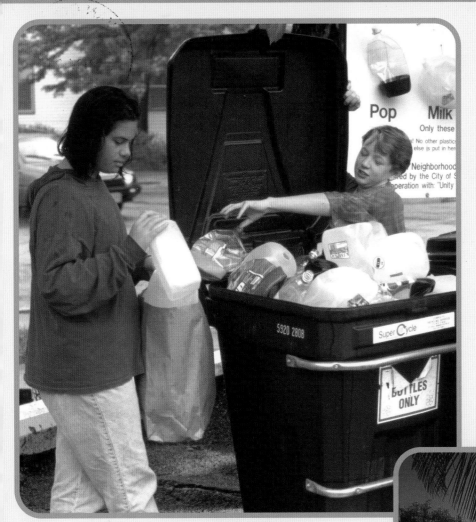

The good news is that most waste contains valuable materials that can be used again. This is called recycling. Recycling takes a little effort, but it really helps to solve the problem of waste disposal. Everyone can help by recycling and reducing waste.

▲ Taking used bottles, tins and paper to recycling points, so they can be used again, helps to reduce the problem of waste disposal.

## LOOK CLOSER

Litter is any rubbish that is just dumped instead of being disposed of safely. It spoils the look of places and can harm wildlife. Litter causes problems even on tropical islands like the one shown here.

# Household waste

Every one of us has produced all sorts of waste since we got up this morning. It's not just the wrappers we put in the bin – we also produce waste each time we turn on the computer or brush our teeth.

In rich countries, each home produces at least a dustbin-full of rubbish each week. A lot of this is food packaging, such as tins and bottles. We also throw away leftover food, newspapers, clothes and garden clippings. Machines we use in the home, like computers, run on electricity. Often, this has been made in power stations that create harmful waste.

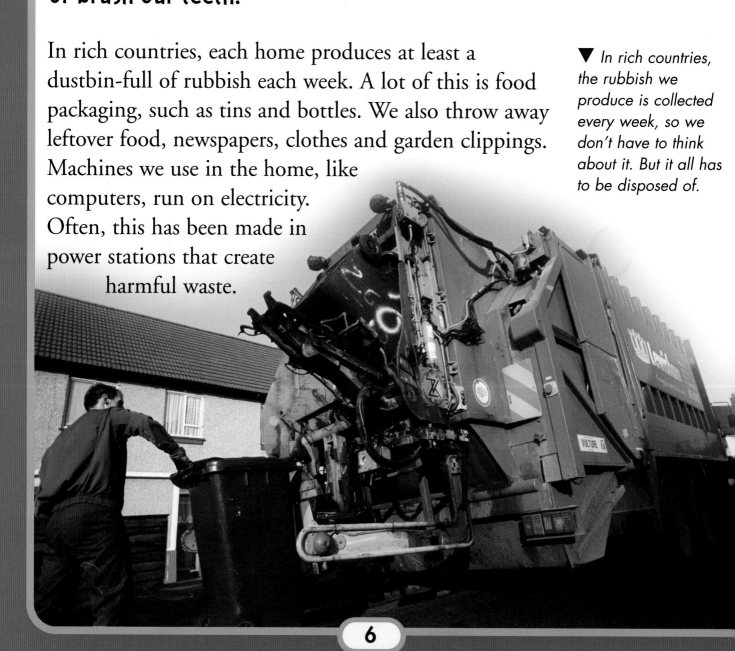

▼ In rich countries, the rubbish we produce is collected every week, so we don't have to think about it. But it all has to be disposed of.

other 7%
food 7%
wood 7%
glass 7%
metal 8%
plastic 8%
plants 18%
paper 38%

As well as the rubbish in the bin, we produce waste water whenever we wash ourselves, our clothes or dishes or go to the toilet. In rich countries, some of this dirty water is cleaned in sewage plants, so it is safe to use again. In poorer countries, the polluted water often empties into lakes and rivers, where it can do harm to wildlife.

▲ *The rubbish we throw away each week is roughly made up of these percentages of waste. Most of it can be recycled.*

## CLOSE TO HOME

Batteries used to power radios, torches and personal stereos are made from chemicals. These produce poisonous waste that lasts for many centuries. If dumped carelessly, batteries harm nature, but they can now be recycled.

# Problem packaging

**M**uch of the rubbish we throw away each week is food packaging, mainly cardboard cartons but also tins and bottles. In the last 20 years or so, the food we buy from supermarkets has come with more and more packaging. This adds to the problem of waste disposal.

In poorer countries, people buy fresh foods grown locally from the nearest market. In rich countries, supermarkets sell foods from all over the world. These goods are packaged to keep them safe on the long trip to the supermarket and to make them look more attractive.

◀ *It is great fun getting new toys. Often, though, these products come in lots of packaging and have been made in faraway countries.*

## CLOSE TO HOME

Next time your family goes shopping, have a look at all the packaging. For example, clothes often have just one layer of packaging, breakfast cereals have several layers and fancy goods, like a box of chocolates, have the most of all.

▼ *Bright packaging on supermarket shelves is designed to tempt us to buy the products.*

Packaging is often made from valuable materials: cardboard is made from trees, glass from minerals and plastic from oil. Energy is used to make packaging, and the process may cause pollution. In addition, transporting goods uses fuel, which creates pollution.

# Waste disposal

**H**ave you ever wondered what happens to the waste that is collected from your dustbin? It usually ends up in large pits called landfills, like 90 per cent of the world's waste.

At landfills, rubbish is packed down, then regularly covered with layers of soil. When the pit is full, a thicker layer of soil is added. Then the site may be reused as a park or golf course. The problem is that many countries are running out of land that can be used for landfills.

◀ *A lorry tips its load of rubbish into a landfill. Sometimes poisonous chemicals leak out from these sites to pollute nearby land.*

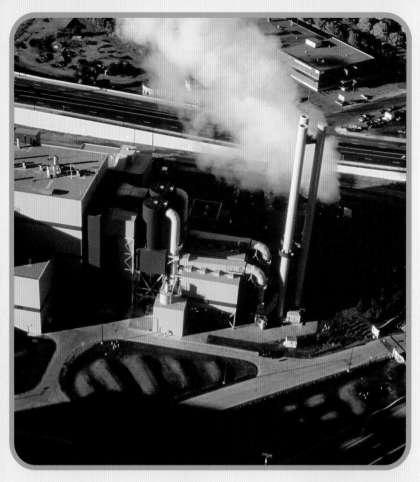

Rotting rubbish gives off a gas called methane. Pipes are sunk into landfills to release this gas. It can then be used as fuel. Rubbish itself can also provide fuel. It is sometimes burned in huge ovens called incinerators, and the heat is used to generate electricity. However, the incinerators produce a lot of ash that still has to be buried in landfills.

▲ *The oven in an incinerator must be very hot to burn plastic. If it is too cool, poisonous gases called dioxins are released.*

## LOOK CLOSER

At small biogas plants like this one in Africa, grass, dung and water are mixed to produce manure and methane. The manure is used to fertilise fields. The methane provides energy for cooking.

# Rotten rubbish

**S**ome types of rubbish biodegrade, or rot, quickly. Other waste, mainly man-made materials, take hundreds of years to decay or don't rot at all.

Things made from natural materials, such as paper, wood, wool and cotton, rot quickly. They are said to be biodegradable. When plants and animals die, their remains are eaten and broken down by worms, beetles, fungi and tiny bacteria. This process returns the goodness that the dead plants and animals contain to the soil, where it nourishes more plants.

▶ In a woodland, nothing goes to waste. Animals, such as deer, eat plants. When they die, plants and animals are eaten by minibeasts, fungi and bacteria.

Artificial materials, such as plastic, metal and glass, aren't biodegradable – they don't decay or decay very slowly. This makes them useful as building or storage materials, but it becomes a problem when we want to throw them away. Most of these materials, however, can be reused or recycled, so they shouldn't just be thrown away.

## LOOK CLOSER

The litter you see on beaches provides a clue to the materials that rot and don't rot quickly. Next time you visit a beach, look to see what kinds of litter are washed up.

◀ Plastic litter spoils the landscape until someone clears it up.

# Farm waste

Farms produce a lot of waste that rots quickly. On traditional farms, it is recycled. However, many modern farms now produce waste that does not decay and is highly poisonous.

Farms produce natural waste, such as leftover plant stems and animal dung. This waste decays quickly to form manure, which is useful. Farmers traditionally spread manure on their fields as fertiliser. Farms that use this method reduce their waste.

▼ A tractor sprays manure on fields to fertilise them. In this way, waste is used again.

▶ *A helicopter sprays chemical pesticides onto fields to kill pests, such as insects.*

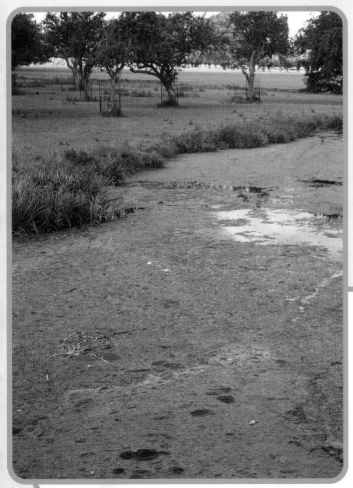

In rich countries, many farms now use chemicals instead of manure as fertiliser. This method produces bumper crops but causes a waste-disposal problem. The leftover chemicals pollute the soil and water supplies and harm animals.

## LOOK CLOSER

Tiny plants called algae thrive in water polluted by fertiliser or waste water from houses. As the algae grow, they make the water green and cloudy. When sunlight cannot filter through the water, animals, such as fish, suffer. The algae also use up all the water's oxygen, which harms water life.

# Industrial waste

**M**ines, factories and power stations produce far more waste than all the buildings in crowded cities. Solid, liquid and gas waste from industry may pollute the air, water or land.

The mining of metals and fuel is vital for industry and manufacturing. However, when metals are mined, a huge amount of waste rock and dust is left behind. This waste, called tailings, contains metals and other substances that pollute the landscape. The factories that process the raw materials also produce a lot of waste.

▼ This bauxite mine in Venezuela has been built on rainforest land. Waste from the mine harms forest life.

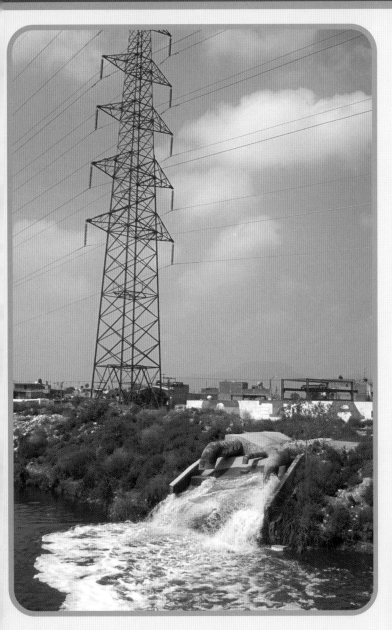

Power stations burn fuels to make electricity. In the process, they release waste gases, such as carbon dioxide, into the air. These gases act as a blanket that traps the Sun's heat near Earth's surface. This is causing Earth's climate to get warmer, an effect known as global warming.

◄ *Liquid waste from a factory in Mexico pollutes the local canal.*

## CLOSE TO HOME

Tins that contain fizzy drinks are usually made of steel or a light, strong metal called aluminium. Aluminium is made from a mineral called bauxite. Tropical forests and other wild areas are being cleared to make way for new bauxite mines. When this happens, local wildlife is destroyed.

# Dangerous waste

Some factories and power stations produce toxic, or poisonous, waste that is very difficult to get rid of. These poisons remain dangerous for hundreds, even thousands, of years.

Nuclear waste is one of the most dangerous types of waste. The rays it gives off can kill people and wildlife. Nuclear waste is produced by power stations, which use a metal called uranium to make energy. Less dangerous waste from these power stations is released into the air or buried at sea. The most deadly waste is stored underground in sealed drums.

◀ *A worker shifts a drum containing nuclear waste at a special burial site in the United States.*

◀ *When toxic waste is dumped at sea, it often leaks and builds up in the bodies of large creatures, such as beluga whales, killing them.*

Factories that make paint, soap, cosmetics, plastic, fertilisers and medicines also produce toxic waste. If this is buried underground, it sometimes seeps into local water supplies and makes people sick. Some towns built on these sites have been torn down after people living there became ill.

## LOOK CLOSER

Old-style refrigerators contain dangerous chemicals called chlorofluorocarbons (CFCs), which harm the layer of ozone gas high in the air that screens us from harmful rays in sunlight. CFCs were banned in 1987, and new refrigerators don't contain them. This ban has had some effect on restoring ozone. CFCs have to be removed from old fridges. Often there are stockpiles of worn-out fridges waiting for this to happen.

# Rich or poor

Some countries produce more waste than others. People from wealthy regions, like the United States and Europe, generally create far more waste than people from poorer places, such as India and Africa.

Rich countries produce a lot of waste partly because people living there have more money to spend on new products. When machinery breaks down, it is often easier to throw it away rather than get it repaired. We also use energy wastefully. Rich countries are now concerned about pollution and waste disposal, and some governments have introduced strict laws to control pollution.

◀ Heavily packaged foods like chips, burgers and soft drinks are very popular in rich countries.

In poorer parts of the world, people have less money to spend on new goods, so they reuse and repair things. Recycling is a way of life. Cardboard, plastic and bottles are all carefully cleaned, sorted and used again. However, pollution controls are often less strict, so some towns, farms and factories release dangerous waste into the environment.

▲ *In poor countries, some people earn a living rummaging through rubbish at landfills in search of things to sell or reuse.*

## LOOK CLOSER

In various parts of the world, people use and throw away very different amounts of paper. The average person in the United States uses over 300 kg of paper in a year. In Britain, people use only about half that amount: 165 kg. In India, the figure is only 3 kg.

UK

USA

India

# Recycling waste

**A**ll the waste we throw away is steadily building up to clutter and harm our planet. What can be done about it? Recycling is part of the answer to the growing problem of waste.

▲ A truck dumps a load of broken glass, called cullet, for recycling. Beforehand, the glass is sorted into different colours, which are melted down separately.

Recycling not only cuts down on waste but can also save energy and useful resources. Glass is easy to recycle. It is made by melting sand and limestone in a furnace. Recycled glass is smashed up and then reheated. This process uses less energy than making new glass and helps to save sand and limestone.

Paper and cardboard are also easy to recycle. These are made from wood. Trees that provide wood for paper are grown in special plantations, often on land that was once wild heath or marshland. Recycling paper helps to save trees and wild land. It also saves energy, which is used when trees are felled and wood is made into paper.

▼ A forester prepares timber for transport to the sawmill, where it will be pulped for paper.

Paper and cardboard can be reused at home, as well as recycled. Envelopes can be reused by putting a gummed label over the address. Old Christmas and birthday cards can be made into gift tags. Always write on both sides of a sheet of paper before recycling it.

# Reuse or recycle

Clothes, metal and plastic can all be recycled to ease the problem of waste disposal. Always think if something can be repaired or reused before throwing it in the bin!

Metals, such as iron, steel and aluminium, can be recycled any number of times. The used metal is simply reheated and remoulded to make new objects, from steel girders to paper clips. The process cuts down on waste and pollution from mining and saves energy. For example, making tins from recycled steel only uses a quarter of the energy used to make tins from fresh steel.

◄ At recycling plants, plastic is shredded into tiny pieces before being melted down and used again.

◀ *In poor countries, where metal is prized, people are skilled at finding new uses for metal objects. This man is sitting on a steel chair made from old tyre rims.*

## CLOSE TO HOME

Many products have symbols printed on them that show that they can be recycled. Next time you go shopping, look for recycling symbols, such as the ones shown below. They all mean that the packaging can be recycled.

Old clothes can also be recycled. They are ripped apart and cleaned. The recycled fibres can then be woven into new cloth or used to stuff mattresses. Plastic is harder to recycle, as there are many different kinds that cannot be mixed together. However, an amazing number of objects can now be made from recycled plastic. For example, fleece jackets can be made from plastic bottles.

# How can we help?

**W**e can all help to tackle the problem of waste by following the three 'Rs': Reduce, Reuse and Recycle. Reduce waste by buying goods with less packaging. Reuse items, such as glass jars and plastic bags. Recycle the rest!

Nowadays, many countries have set up recycling schemes to save resources and reduce the amount of waste they have to deal with. Governments have also made laws to cut waste pollution from farms and factories. Campaign groups, such as Greenpeace, have helped to stop the dumping of poisonous waste.

◀ Old newspapers can be collected and taken to a recycling bin. Never throw them away!

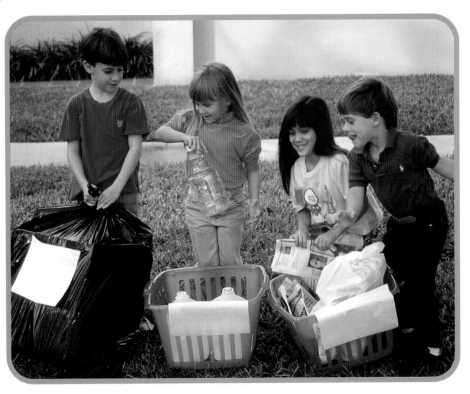

Take advantage of local schemes by recycling used paper, card, metal, plastic, glass and clothes. Clean these materials and bag them. Take old toys, books and clothes to charity shops, where they can be resold to raise money. When you go shopping, look out

▲ *Recycling takes a bit more time, but if we all do it, it will really help to reduce waste.*

for labels that show items are made using recycled materials, such as toilet rolls. Reuse things like plastic bags or glass jars, too.

In the garden, start a compost heap using old wooden boxes or a dustbin with holes drilled in the bottom. Put in natural waste, like vegetable peelings, which will rot on the heap to make a rich compost. This can then be used to fertilise flowers.

◀ *The waste on a compost heap decays, forming a natural fertiliser.*

# Waste projects

**I**nvestigate the types of rubbish that decay quickly and those that don't by carrying out the simple experiment shown here. You can also use old newspapers, cardboard, plastic pots, corks and balloons to make beautiful masks.

▲ *Natural materials, such as apples, decay quickly. They are broken down by minibeasts and bacteria.*

### WILL IT ROT?

Find out more about the kinds of rubbish that do and don't rot by burying rubbish in pots. You could use old yogurt pots or flowerpots.

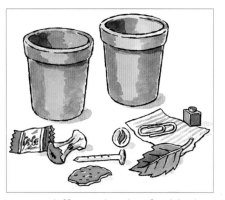

1. Put different kinds of rubbish in each pot. Include natural materials, such as fruit, vegetable peelings, wood or paper. Put man-made materials, such as a small plastic toy or a crisp packet, glass marbles and metal screws in other pots.

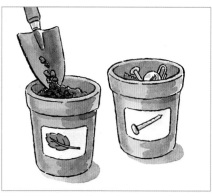

2. Use a trowel to cover each item of rubbish with damp soil, then store the pots in a damp place outside. Label each pot to show what it contains.

3. After a month, remove the soil to find out which items have decayed. Has anything disappeared altogether? What has happened to the metal? Are there any changes to the glass or plastic? Write down your results in a notebook.

## MAKING MASKS FROM JUNK

Use rubbish, including old newspapers and plastic pots, to make masks for yourself and your friends, perhaps for a party. You will also need paste made from flour and water, scissors, a balloon, elastic and poster paints.

1. The basic masks are made from papier-mâché. Blow up a balloon and tear newspaper into strips. Soak the strips in paste and cover the balloon with at least four layers of strips.

2. Leave the papier-mâché for a day or two, until completely dry. Now pop the balloon. Cut the papier-mâché ball in half to make two masks. Measure and cut holes for your eyes and mouth.

3. Plan your mask: it could be an animal, a clown or a pirate. Cover the papier-mâché with several layers of paint. Glue on card or plastic strips for ears, teeth and a tongue and stick on a plastic pot or cork for the nose.

**Ask an adult to help you when using scissors.**

### CAMPAIGN GROUPS

Friends of the Earth
26–28 Underwood Street, London
N1 7JQ
Website: www.foe.co.uk

Greenpeace
Canonbury Villas, London N1 2PN
Website: www.greenpeace.org

WWF: Panda House, Weyside Park
Godalming, Surrey GU7 1XR
Website: www.wwf.org.uk

### WASTE AND RECYCLING WEBSITES

US Environment Protection Agency: www.epa.gov/students
Environment explorers' club: www.epa.gov/kids
Wastewatch UK: www.wastewatch.org.uk

### OTHER INFORMATION WEBSITES

www.georesources.co.uk
www.thomasrecycling.com/kids.html
Kids recycling: www.kidsrecycle.org
Waste quiz: www.pca.state.mn.us/kids/kidsQuizGarbage.cfm

# Waste factfile

• In the 1970s, a former landfill site called Love Canal near Niagara Falls in the United States hit the news. In the 1950s, a housing estate and school were built on the site. Then people there began to get sick. The site was found to be poisoned by waste, and the estate had to be pulled down.

• The worst disaster involving nuclear waste happened at a site called Kyshtym in Russia in 1957. An explosion at a nuclear storage site scattered radioactive waste over a vast region covering 15 000 sq km. Full details of the accident are not known, but hundreds of people probably died.

• In 1975, an American company called the Minnesota Mining and Manufacturing Company launched a campaign called "Pollution Prevention Pays" to reduce waste. It put into practice 1200 ideas for cutting waste and pollution. Ten years later, it had halved its waste production and saved nearly 500 million dollars.

• The United States produces more waste than any other country. With only 5 per cent of the world's population, it produces 19 per cent of the world's waste. However, it is better at recycling than many other countries. It recycles a quarter of its domestic waste, whereas Britain, for example, only manages 12 per cent.

• Steel is the world's most recycled metal. The steel produced today is made from about 40 per cent recycled metal.

# Glossary

**Biodegradable**
A biodegradable substance rots, for example, plant and animal waste.

**Bacteria**
Microscopic single-celled life forms.

**Biogas**
A gas given off by plant and animal waste as they rot.

**Cullet**
Smashed glass that can be remelted to make new glass.

**Fuel**
A substance that can be burned to release energy in the form of light and heat.

**Global warming**
Warming weather worldwide, caused by the increase of gases in the air, such as carbon dioxide, that trap the Sun's heat.

**Incinerator**
A very hot furnace in which rubbish is burned, often to generate electricity.

**Landfill**
A pit in the ground where rubbish is dumped and then covered with earth.

**Methane**
A gas given off by rotting rubbish, which can be burned to provide energy.

**Mineral**
A non-living chemical substance.

**Non-biodegradable**
A non-biodegradable substance does not rot, for example, plastic and glass.

**Pesticides**
Chemicals that farmers spray on fields to kill crop-harming pests, such as insects.

**Pollution**
Harmful waste substances.

**Radioactive**
A radioactive material gives off dangerous radiation.

**Recycling**
The process of reclaiming useful materials from waste. They are either used again or made into new products.

**Resources**
Materials, such as wood, oil and metal, that are used to make things.

**Sewage plant**
Place where used, dirty water is filtered and cleaned so it is safe and can be used again.

# Index